NATIONAL GEOGRAPHIC
Young Explorer!

Fly With a
Butterfly 2

A Butterfly Is Born

Spring is here.
So are butterflies.

A **butterfly** sits on a plant.
She lays an **egg**.

butterfly

A butterfly egg is small.
It will hatch soon.
A **caterpillar** will come out.

egg

The caterpillar is hungry.
It eats the plant.
The caterpillar grows.

caterpillar

The caterpillar hangs
from a plant.
It starts to change.

caterpillar

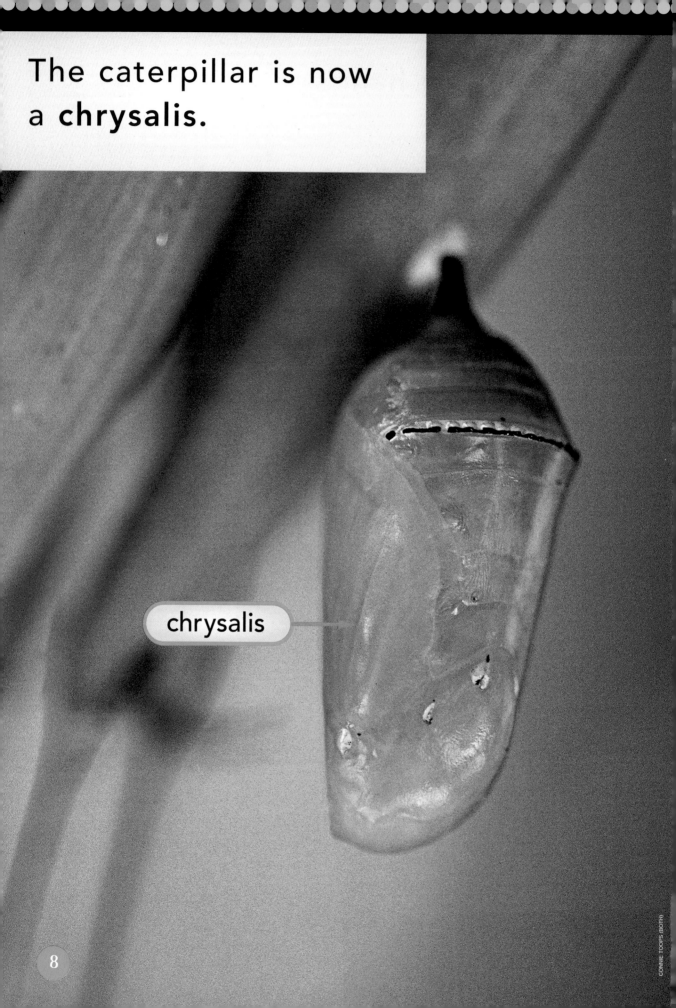

The caterpillar is now a **chrysalis.**

chrysalis

It keeps changing.
It grows wings.
Now it is a butterfly.

butterfly

The butterfly's wings are soft.
They grow bigger.
Then they get hard.

butterfly

wings

The butterfly flies away.

A Butterfly Grows

How does a butterfly grow?

Look at the drawing.

Follow each step.

6 The butterfly flies away.

5 The chrysalis becomes a butterfly.

PRECISION GRAPHICS

4 It turns into a chrysalis.

1 A butterfly starts as an egg.

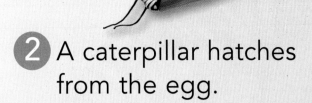

2 A caterpillar hatches from the egg.

3 The caterpillar hangs from a plant.

Compare the Parts

How are a caterpillar and a butterfly alike?

How are they different?

Caterpillar

head

front antenna

back antenna

legs

CONNIE TOOPS

Butterfly

head

antenna

legs

© GARY BELL/OCEANWIDE IMAGES.COM

wings

How Seeds

spread

Seeds **spread** in many ways.
How does this girl spread seeds?

seed

How does a **plant** spread **seeds?**

How does water spread seeds?

seed

19

How does a dog spread seeds?

seed

seed

How does a chipmunk spread seeds?
What else spreads seeds?

butterfly

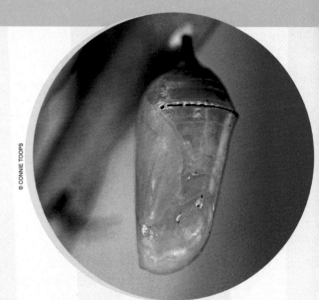

chrysalis

caterpillar

egg

plant

© BIOS/KLEIN & HUBERT/PETER ARNOLD

spread

seed

NATIONAL
GEOGRAPHIC
Young
Explorer!

Butterfly

She finds a spot. Her stay is brief.
She lays her egg beneath a leaf.

Inside the egg, day after day,
A caterpillar has a way

Of knowing how to stretch and grow.
Once on her own, she likes to show

The kind of trick that nature brings
When she spreads her WINGS!

—J. Patrick Lewis

NATIONAL GEOGRAPHIC Young Explorer!

DEVELOPMENT TEAM
Vice President and Publisher:
  Francis Downey
Art Director and Designer:
  Karen Thompson
Editor and Writer: Sara Chauhan
Editor: Macon Morehouse
Digital Editor: Shelby Alinsky
Digital Designer: Ryan Ford
Photo Editors: Mary Ann Price
  Shannon Hibberd
Permissions Editor: Jean Cantu
Production Specialist:
  Dreama Karnes-Bynane

SCHOOL PUBLISHING GROUP
President and Chief Executive Officer:
  Alison Wagner
Research Manager: Christina An

MANUFACTURING AND QUALITY CONTROL
Chief Financial Officer:
  Christopher A. Liedel
Sr. Vice President: Phillip L. Schlosser
Director: Clifton M. Brown
Manager: Nicole Elliott
Postal Director: Kerry Knight

PUBLISHED BY THE
NATIONAL GEOGRAPHIC SOCIETY
John M. Fahey, Jr., *Chairman and C*
Timothy T. Kelly, *President*

NATIONAL GEOGRAPHIC
YOUNG EXPLORER (ISSN 1930-8116)
is published seven times during the school
year—September, October, November–
December, January–February, March, Apri
May—by the National Geographic Society
1145 17th Street NW, Washington, D.C.
20036–4688. Postmaster: Please send add
changes to National Geographic Explorer,
Box 4002865, Des Moines, IA 50340–05
Periodical postage paid at Washington, D
and additional mailing offices.

To subscribe:
  In the U.S., call 1-888-915-3276
  In Australia and New Zealand,
    + 61 2 8005 6889
  In China, + 86 10 6493 4469
  In Hong Kong, + 852 2191 2518
  In Malaysia, + 60 3 2782 0243
  In Singapore, + 65 6744 9888

Cover: A monarch butterfly rests on a flo
(Photo by Tom and Pat Leeson)

05/13/QGWA/2

FIND US ONLINE